Shadow and Praise

In praise of you!

poems by

Terry Wolverton

Terry Wolverton

MAIN STREET RAG PUBLISHING COMPANY
CHARLOTTE, NORTH CAROLINA

Cover art by: Emmanuelle Purdon/Collection: Digital Vision/Getty Images

Acknowledgements:

Poems in this collection have appeared previously in *Prairie Schooner, Eclipse, The Columbia Poetry Review, The Del Sol Review,* and *writersatwork.com.*

The author would like to thank the members of the Women's Poetry Project, who shepherded these poems, and especially Julia Cole and Gwin Wheatley, who reviewed the manuscript.

Library of Congress Control Number: 2007920100

ISBN: 978-1-59948-057-2
ISBN: 1-59948-057-3

Produced in the United States of America

Main Street Rag
4416 Shea Lane
Charlotte, NC 28227
www.MainStreetRag.com

dedicated to the memory
of Arlene Raven
1944-2006

Contents

Terry Wolverton

Introduction

It's easy to see why Terry Wolverton has a reputation as a right-on facilitator of writing workshops: I couldn't find a wasted word in these poems in spite of the rhetorical amplification that governs many of them, nor a threadbare syllogism in the often staccato, sometimes surreal thought-processes along which we are guided. The short "Shadow" section takes the self, the subjectivity, and the Other as objects of phenomenological (and Lacanian) investigation under the aspects of Specter, Surveillance, Photophobia, Groundhog, Death, and Paradox. It de-familiarizes the proverbial Shadows of A Doubt, of Shadow-Boxing, of Your Smile, of Me and My Shadow, and of the Five O'Clock Beard. The transitional "difficult praise" does indeed lead us to litanies of praise for what no one this side of Whitman has a good word for—e.g. Denial, Ultraviolet Rays, Pandora's Box, Bad Drivers, and Traffic on the 405 Freeway—as well as original takes on what everyone else praises but without Terry's angular, elliptical, imaginative inner eye: e.g. Blueberries, The Senses, Heaven, Green, Living, Singing, Flowers. Eventually she finds the cosmic (and cosmically comic) capacity to praise both "everyone" and "anyone," not to mention "nothing." These poems vibrate with controlled breathing, like American Mantras infused by a higher plane of Eastern Scriptural Spirituality. I have the highest admiration for this achievement by a poet and human being who has spent a lifetime in preparation for such a crowning masterpiece. It's been said that some are Poets Born and others Poets Made. Terry Wolverton is both. *Shadows and Praise* is a Himalayan Peak rising from the asphalt desert (and I love deserts) of Southern California. Yet it is start-to-finish in the accessible language that has always, for me at least, constituted the most enjoyable and rewarding tradition within SoCal poetry and, indeed, American Literature.

Gerald Locklin
Professor Emeritus of English
California State University, Long Beach

Shadow

"…shadow seeks shadow…"

— H.D.

Specter

Born in Bomb's shadow, atomic dust
still making the rounds, optimism
a lapsed fashion, white panties smirched in
global gangbang, *wham bam*, for what was
I born to hope, ducked and covering
my moist shame. Two flag-draped blasts seared our
shadows onto crusts of history.
Now we are ghost ships drifting through this
lost century. How do we woo back
the sun we mocked, how mend our broken
continents? Shadows chasing shadows.
Nuclear tribe, what nucleus will
bind us now—our death tango, mute howls,
amnesia's convenient balm?

Under Surveillance

My suitcases have arrived without
me, clatter into a room furbished
with suspicion, unpack themselves.
Dresses suspend their silky weight on
wire arms of hangers; headless hats
rack brains in airless cupboards. Unseen,
I crouch in shadow, watch through distant
keyhole, intrepid spy in the house
of my own life—aloof in trenchcoat,
Emma Peel boots. Watch how the books fan
their pages in evening breeze, how
my pajamas sigh into cool sheets.
No fingerprints engrave the doorknob;
on the pillow, no imprint of dreams.

Groundhog Day

On days too dark to see my shadow
I walk forlorn, unable to recall
my silhouette. Slate sidewalks mirror
nothing but my doubt: am I here or
is light streaming through me? Has my form,
once dense, dissolved, molecules broadcast
like billiard balls after a clean break?
Fingers probe the putty of the face,
as if to reconfirm its relevance,
find vacant sockets. Once I was twinned,
dusky umbra floating always by
my side. Severed now from that consoling
double, my half-life skitters over
shattered pavement, seeking its bass note.

Photophobia

I suckled darkness. Alone, crib-bound,
I learned a thirst for it, clamped down on
pessimism's wizened tit. Fattened
on its putrid trickle, cradled in
blues. Soon I chafed against the bruising
softness—my mother's arms, the shipwrecked
ambiguities that pass for love.
I strapped a scabbard on my chalky
hips, skewered daybreak. I court tango,
guzzle rum, ride subways past midnight.
Don't ask me to be happy. That's me
behind Ray-Bans, corner slumped, rocked to
end of line. Me, huddled over black
coffee, crooning "Shadow of Your Smile."

Shadow of Doubt

I live inside a revolving door
where certainty unravels with the
predictability of trains. All
night long, Harpies croon through subway grates,
songs of malice and regret. Their dust
breath filters city stars, pinholes in
indigo. I used to navigate
by stars. Now bindings unstitch, seams split,
I twirl empty as a bell, unstruck,
a page unwriting itself, missed stop
on the milk run, sad shuttered station.
I hum tuneless elevator tunes;
fingers worry the frayed strands bloody.
My reflection in the smoked glass blurs.

Shadow Boxing

God makes promises he cannot keep.
I want to lure him from the dark place
under the stairs; I want to face my
accuser. But gloves jab air, sink in
blubber, paunch of a lazy fuck-off
who never pulls his weeds or bundles
trash, who litters the roadside with his
mistakes. I'm one. Knuckles bleed inside
leather. I live between the temples
but forget to worship. I do my
best to tongue these broken consonants,
but my continents drift tonight. Just
when I am overcome with the taste
of light, I'm slammed to canvas, bell sounds.

Shadow of Your Smile

You make me want to change my blouse, give
up midnight to sigh beside you in
cool sheets. Your blunt hands rearrange my
frequency, quicken cells' vibration
until I can no longer discern
touch from what is touched. I am honey
swirling helpless into bone teacups.
I'm just a whore for approval. Have
I hung my mirrors 'round your neck? Crumbs
of sweetness pool in my collarbone.
I'm sewn to you now, gestures mirror
yours. Who echoes whom? Which is the source
of light? Your weapon glimmers like the
fickle moon by which I am eclipsed.

Me and My Shadow

The other girl nobody sees, hair
smeared with shit, tongue too large for her mouth.
striking matches behind the garage,
masturbating under basement stairs.
All night she spies on my sleep, sucks dreams
from the indigo soup. Radio
lulls her with Harpy songs. She waltzes
alone, dead cat in wire arms. Plants small
bombs in china teacups, watches while
honey burns. Behind fanned fingers, girls
gossip, aim their knife points at her hunched
spine. She scrapes them off like barnacles,
toughens her hull, continues to sail
unseen through dark waters, a ghost ship.

Five O'Clock Shadow

Some August evening, you'll notice
the shortening light, sun surrendered
to purpling hills, summer revoked
like a lover's promise. Even breeze
smells different, one more sign you've been
ignoring until just this moment,
a moment that contains all endings.
We can't hide from our darkness. Patient,
it will wait all day to bloom on our
chins, erase our masks of innocence,
or steal pavement's heat. Then we crouch in
color-starved twilight, puny candles
held aloft. Umbra lengthens as we
search for the blade to scrape our souls clean.

Shadow of Death

Sometimes I can feel death coming, as
an afternoon grows still before earth
quakes. A certain smell of dust, the taste
of water trembling in a glass.
I hear my cells decode the body's
cryptogram, unstring its DNA
like blind syllables. Sometimes I climb
rooftops, call death's name, summon lightning
from night's velvet pocket. "Come and get
me," I taunt, tangoing on rail's edge.
I wear traces of ash under my
fingernails; this way death can't sneak up
behind me, snap my control, stuff me
in his suitcase when I'm not looking.

Paradox

In the midst of singing is silence,
small gaps of breath. The billowed lung soon
empties of its air. Every thing
contains its opposite: Love changes
its blouse to emerge as loathing; good
fortune shrivels to despair. That star
we yearn toward is the radiance
we fear. Haunted by what we've escaped,
we cling to overstuffed suitcases
that open to reveal the void
we carry everywhere. Shadow
can't survive without the sun's bright beam,
and Death keeps Life in its coat pocket;
fingers stroke it like a lucky charm.

difficult praise

easy to praise the hummingbird
harder to extol rat, corpse splayed
on walking path beside the reservoir

effortless to laud ardent sun
more difficult to bow to brush fire's
scarred ground, cremated juniper

easy to cheer poem that bares the world behind the world
easier still to curse slammed door of rejection note—
third one this month

natural to exalt warm flesh of the beloved
but how to honor one who leaves
you to rattle through empty days?

god's fingerprints are everywhere—
hot jazz, bad drivers
malignant tumor and first snowfall
cats' paws, crooked politicians

help me learn to praise it all,
open my heart to every
blessed thing

Praise

"Some praise at morning what they blame at night…"

Alexander Pope

In praise of denial

Acts unwreak themselves, as the skeleton disarticulates with time. In the chambered brain, dendrites spark like downed power lines; whole neighborhoods go dark. Sputtering candles cast shadows in cluttered rooms; we forget what dwells within these walls, outlines of furniture no longer sharp. Charred arm of sofa blurs; bullet hole near kitchen sink scabs over. Scar at temple fades, bruises retreat underground. Soon a whole life sinks back into medulla's soup and, though I have no clue how I got here, I am swimming in a warm blue sea. Breezes whisper something I can't catch. Nothing hurts now. Sun streaming like a benediction.

In praise of sun

Especially at this time of year, long shadows of December afternoon, fires cooling finally, pale light a fickle promise. Orange candle glow is cold consolation for five o'clock darkness. Stricken with S.A.D., vitamin D deprived. Though I dwell in California, I dream of Miami, Havana, Baja Sur. I will follow that hot yellow star wherever she migrates, topsy-turvy world under equator. I will make my humble skin an altar, anointed, offer it up for worship. Drink light's nectar into every pore. Invoke coronae, solar flares. Court ultraviolet and refute all possibility of melanoma. After all, the sun is my mother; how can the one who gives life ever do you harm?

In praise of mother

She, who taught you the habit of intimacy, habit you either have or have not kicked. "You have your mother's hands," observes the lover who tells you, on a train, that she is done. Not the romantic night train of French movies but flat Midwestern Amtrak in the final desolate week of December. Frozen wheat fields scabbed with old snow chug by as she lets go your hand, lets go your mother's hand, escapes through a hole in the future. Your mother will nod in baleful recognition because, after all, she schooled you in such habits of intimacy. Then she will crow, "See, you're not happy either," triumphant that her apple still clings to its tree. Her eyes that glow with love and hunger, as if to devour and thus reabsorb the life she gave you. After all, you owe her; her fissuring became your gateway to the future.

In praise of future

Isn't its chief virtue that it hasn't yet occurred? Forget those quantum quacks who insist all time is simultaneous, the movie *and* its sequels at the same multiplex. Tomorrow winks at us, all fickle promise and allure. Most of us still clamor to believe its flimflam sleight of hand, its mumbo jumbo mirrors, smoky hocus-pocus. We line up for the skin game. We're convinced that, like weather, the future happens *to* us, fancy ourselves innocent bystanders. Fate, we shrug and sigh. *Que sera, sera.* Though it makes us crazy not to know. The mystery that captivates is also foe; we pledge to undermine our innocence. Consult hand-painted decks and crystal balls, seek out celestial cartographers. We train our eyes to burn through mirror, see to the other side. All in an effort to spoil the surprise.

In praise of surprise

To offset the disappointment of *knowing*, we are offered the terror of surprise. To be surprised means to be caught unaware, panties around ankles, vigilance lapsed. Eye in the back of one's head dozing. Dereliction. Relief. Lidless eye turned inwards, a child burrowed under blankets, unseeing, presumed unseen. Blankets sweet with night's secretions, musty wool. What's unseen we might suppose unseeable, but we'd be wrong. This shocks us; we'd imagined we were all alone. In darkened living room, thirty people leap from behind furniture to scream "Happy Birthday." It is hours before I stop trembling, before the epinephrine spike subsides. Suddenly I am older and everyone is there to witness. History is written on my face for all to read. My friends are wearing paper hats, and the cake is studded with blueberries.

In praise of blueberries

In the game where you list foods by color, only one comes by its blue honestly. Blue gummy bears, blue Jell-o, blue M&M's—concoctions of the factory. Drenched in Brilliant Blue FCF, synthetic coal tar dye banned in eleven European nations. Blueberries are still found in the wild, in mosquito-y bogs of southwest Michigan on sticky July mornings. Sky heavy, overcast, air clouded with bloodsuckers droning their welcome. Sawbuck in the farmer's pocket; he overlooks your halter top, Hollywood sunglasses, impossible platform shoes, stench of Dior's Poison—concoctions of the factory. Aluminum pail drapes your wrist like a new purse, thumps thigh; later there will be bruises. Surfeit of gems dangle from branches. Too many to gather, so you pop them into mouth. Nothing like the wads of cottony pulp in plastic jewel boxes on supermarket shelves where you come from. Tart stains your tongue.

Terry Wolverton

In praise of supermarkets

No matter how much we buy, the stores will never be empty. This is America. It is a kind of trance, pushing our metal carts down those wide aisles of cake mixes and laundry soap arrayed in pleasing patterns. Twenty-six brands of cereal; nineteen flavors of canned soup. Lurid pyramids of fruit, waxed to gleaming. Crackling packages of frozen vegetables. Soothing assurance of abundance, surfeit. Even in childhood, I'd haunt the bright-lit rows, coins sweaty in my pocket, mesmerized by bags of red-wrapped Kit Kats, yellow Butterfingers. Even now, it's not for sustenance, but entertainment. Alone on a Saturday night, I find myself wheeling a languorous cart past condiments or household cleansers. Humming to Muzak. Flirting mildly with the Ecuadorian checker who sometimes undercharges me. This is America. I wave my little paper flag. There will never be revolution in the U.S. as long as the shelves are stocked.

In praise of revolution

33 1/3 per minute. Is it me, or does our globe spin faster now? Lotus Weinstock quipped that she felt like a piece of shit the whole world revolved around. These days she's turning in her grave. I was a teenage revolutionary. I bought the soundtrack. Let slogans detonate in my mouth. My tongue dissolved the windowpane to a new world. I pledge allegiance to a new axis, begin to spiral. Room blurs, face in mirror a convoluted surprise. Who knows of what I might be capable? Does the music box ballerina believe she twirls free or does she tire of the same bright tune? Or is it vision that whirls away, escapes orbit? People in the streets today, marching. A museum display. A new reality show. Monument to lost time.

In praise of monuments

Where would we be without markers to remind us what's important? Afflicted with collective amnesia, we litter Earth with bronze and marble Post-its. Pillar, column, obelisk, arch. Cardboard box on high shelf preserves plastic poncho, spongy pink curlers, can of chipotle, toy giraffe—detritus of spent love. And photo albums bulge with their panchromatic record, phantom evidence. And my chiseled face, each line a signpost. Time falls and rises, inexorable tide. Impermanence mocks. Dates carved with such precision finally empty of story. Gloves without hands. Graves of the forgotten. Still, granite is cool beneath fingertips; viscera made antiseptic. Stonecutters. we straddle our hunk of rock, tattoo our names onto infinity, claim faith in this flimsy practice of remembering.

In praise of faith

Girlie, everything you know is wrong. Life conspires to dismantle your puny beliefs. Always you have knelt before false gods, made supplication to the unworthy. Scattered your seeds in beds of ash. Bet on the wrong horse. Still you remain steadfast. Buoyed with breath of grace. Study prism'd web in early light. Miracle in the soap dish. Seeds stream through open fingers, drift like ash. You will crown yourself fool again and again and do it willingly. Belief itself a miracle, fragile as soap bubble in these sharp-pointed days. Refuse to root in arid crust of reality. Build your house instead on the fertile plain of illusion. Its walls parchment. Its ceiling of gossamer threads. Inside, a flame burns. Even in sleep, you tend it carefully.

In praise of sleep

I've been awake too long. Darkness bends me over its lap to spank. Only the alarm to referee – it always chimes too soon, too late. My hunger smiles like a sharpened knife. Where is the ship to take me home? I've been wanting the future, but my nightmares keep escaping. When I breathe, when I remember my name. When I trace my fingerprints. My left knee has stopped speaking to its twin, one that genuflects. The kitchen is lethal. Tonight we will devour childhood, a broth thick with old wool. I lie here, sprout bruises. Come morning I spit blood. Sometimes the telephone blasts through my dreams; when I answer, there's nothing but white noise and my own heartbeat. My face changes as I sleep. Tomorrow I won't recognize her when I pick up my shiny spoon.

In praise of spoons

Curved to receive, spoons are gendered. Not hard dick knife, relentless poking tines. Palm scooped to hold. Nurturing hollow, offering cavern. Naked lap. Slotted and demitasse, wooden and soup. Silver feeding. Long-necked ice tea. Beveled grapefruit. Drawerful of anticipation. Ladder of ladles. Big Dipper. Implement defined by its yield. Slip its payload surreptitiously between two lips: Burning swirl of honey, gall of quinine. Shallow bowl of latency. Let us praise the ability to wait, to keep, to hold the breath. Who knows what promise might be fulfilled between unoccupied parentheses?

In praise of parentheses

Some thoughts are better kept to myself. I keep them bundled in a basement cupboard. Beside a bottle of Mercurochrome long dried to rust. Alongside spider carcasses, curled as fists. Under stacks of Polaroids I am compelled to save, though their subjects fade to pale unrecognizable ghosts. Suggestions of form in haloes of dissolved spectrum. Nothing is airtight. No one's built a container time can't escape. Skin is porous. Sometimes thoughts break through the sturdy curvatures I've erected, my cupped palms propped upright. Sometimes they clamber over billowed walls, skitter across page, insert themselves into inopportune sentences. Try to blend in, like any fugitive.

In praise of fugitives

One-armed man could only carry half his weight. I gave up trying twice as hard to disappear into cities of my speculation. Lived brilliant behind dark spectacles. Along the line I went missing. I lost my sense of smell; bloodhounds were restive. Age is the burkha of American women; after fifty we drop off radar, roam boulevards like wild dogs, exiles, escapees. Bandits hoarding sunlight meant for someone else. Dieting down to better fit in shadow's slender gloves. Fugitives maintain a strict agenda: Observe the traffic of stars. Memorize abandoned factories. Keep off of train tracks. Hone story like a lullaby. Remember to breathe. Eschew lipstick.

In praise of lipstick

Shh! Frolic, girl about town. High-strung metropolitan. Crème de la femme craving stiletto frenzy. Strapless visionary tempting carnal x-treme. Seismic B-cup, overload underground odyssey. Underplay underworld fetish. Mischievous voltage, scratch sultry alibi. Reflect pure attitude. Chronic film noir dark side, Lady Danger. Bask hot Tahiti coral reef. Bruise fleshpot, crush love junkie enigma. Real faux, Spanish fly. Desire retro coquette, cherries jubilee. Mystic diva. Love bauble. Touch Uzi impulse, giddy bombshell fusion. Cherish atomic rose, captive metallic sun. Destined meltdown, 3-D exhibitionist myth. Pretty please, pink poodle. Foxy stray dog.

In praise of dogs

Dog in a fireman's hat. Let me go back to live my life in an endless episode of Lassie. Flattest heaven I ever laid eyes on. Will dogs go to heaven? Will I? Whom would I rush into a burning building to save? How many reincarnations have I spent in canine form, led around by my cold, wet nose, unswerving loyalty? After twenty years' absence, Odysseus returned home disguised as a beggar; no one recognized him but his old dog Argus, who wagged his tail, then died. How long must I live leashed to another's intention, their comings and goings? Paws racing through my dreams? With my twilight vision, I can make out the colors of evil. Feel wind stir my hackles; Odin awakes and I begin to howl. Creature of elements, I bury my treasures in earth. Dog loves water, but is afraid of fire.

Terry Wolverton

In praise of fire

I keep praying for spontaneous combustion, but how can lightning strike twice? I always liked to play with matches, out behind the garage. It is better after dark, when end of the world looms. Mesmerized by tracers in night sky, green from night vision photography, I cannot turn my eyes from this incendiary global sitcom. Once lightning was the only source of fire. God hurled the bolts. I choose to be cremated. I long to be consumed. I will walk the red-hot stones to prove my purity. In the next life, let me come back as an arsonist. Let me restore to Vesta her temple of burning, write my opus with scorched fingertips. Hold paper to flame. Disappears like a whisper.

In praise of whispers

Whispers are gusts of forgotten time. They rearrange my brainwaves as I sleep. Scent of iron blows off river, cold breath on my neck. Mist obscures moon. Salt of blood on my tongue. Clanging fills my dreams, wind chimes shuddering. Sister Ignacio of Holy Angels Convent was cautioned never to speak above a whisper. There was never a time she forgot. It is increasingly hard to remember the instructions one receives. Blah blah blah. The harder the wind blows, the easier it is to listen. "Don't speak unless spoken to." Parched lips of silence crack and bleed; the quiet makes my soles itch. From now on she will utter siroccos only; people will call her Twister and hide from her elegant bluster. Whisper captured in a jar will last a thousand years. *Fermé la bouche.* That sealed jar will shatter the need for secrecy. Sister Ignacio opens her parched throat to sigh.

Sister Ignacio offers praise

Under my tongue at night I hold a river stone. I keep it there to quiet my cold sleep. I curl sideways on a mattress of bone. Discordant, I travel my dreams and sometimes bump against furniture. Real or imagined? I'm stumped. Awaken wet, choking, fingernails crusted with dirt. All day I wear hair shirt in secret, beneath the shut of my robes. It muffles crackle of flame that erupts between my thighs when Sister Alouycis' feet clickety-clack across marble floors. Fickle in my devotion, erratic in my vows, sometimes I am lamb, sometimes firecracker. All night I suck river from stone while my eyelids grow parched.

In praise of eyelids

When they excised my blue-veined lids, it grew impossible to sleep. Bare windows, curtains stripped away. Too naked in a too-bright room, no place to hide. Sun bleached color from the furnishings. My worldly goods exposed to strangers' scrutiny. With no place to hide, it grew impossible to sleep. While bean counters probed the content of my dreams. All I owned seeming to dissolve in light. Plundered jewel box of memory. Strange goods exposed to world's scrutiny. Forget me; close the velvet cover. Shroud me in blessed darkness. Forbidden to wink, how will they know when I'm kidding?

In praise of winking

God, when hooded prisoners wag their blue-veined genitals for the camera, are you winking at us? Do you intend to say, "Invest in this spinning ball of dirt and you'll know the real meaning of Hell?" Or do you want us to love this world against all probability, even as its molecules come unbound, dissolving to over-priced dust? Is that the cosmic joke, that what we hold most closely dissipates beneath our grainy fingers? Maybe you have no intention, a random tic of orbicularis oculi. Or merely lapsed attention, an unscheduled nap in galactic twilight. Wake up. When these prisoners scrounge the crapper for their daily rations, I hope you're watching. Send us a signal, one pregnant lowered lid. It wouldn't be the right time to turn your eyes away.

In praise of pregnancy

Fifty-year-old mother-to-be, knocked up by my own exaggerated expectations, my greedy longings. I will name this offspring Outrage, raise her to be an enemy of the state. Scrambled from eggs long past their expiration date, she'll have lidless eyes, cursed to see too much. Nursed at my bitter trough, she'll wear green and inherit my inability to whistle. I'll take her out in a shopping cart, bunkered in bubble wrap. Her first words will be "lopsided" and "careening" and "tormented lust." At thirteen, she'll run away to join a traveling band of all-girl arsonists, return stinking of singed hair. She'll be my pride and joy. She'll be the death of me. Once a year, we'll stand in the front yard and smash our television, like Pandora's box.

In praise of Pandora's box

Hope was not quick enough to join the jailbreak. Her punkass cousins split at the first crack of daylight. Provoked a fracas that swarms the planet still. That's why I always sign my name with spit. It being her nature, she made the best of prolonged captivity. Grew accustomed to the scent of cedar, sedentary lifestyle. Taught herself to knit. Wingbone needles in her small hands. She yoked a sweater of resignation to replace her original plumage. Now it's all the rage on the runway. That's why I speak in my father's stutter. Someday, she thinks, her hapless guardian might lift the lid again. Her walls grow redolent of wool. Needles clack like bones. Hope knits.

In praise of knitting

However it may appear, nothing is straightforward. Always a tangle, a twist, slip knot turning wrist to wrest my grasp on simplicity. Complicit, I drop stitches too. Gasp. Knit one. Purl two. Nine perfect rows before the pattern switches and I am ribbing. Then I make my home in a new motif. No relief until a wave of worsted undulates across my weathered lap, spills forward to lap my toes. Fevered in summertime, blanket of seed stitch and cable. Troubled hands possessed, I cast on (and on) but where do I bind off? I've lost the thread. Forehead puckers. Days unravel, wasted skein. Lulled by needles' tick. Needles prick my torpid senses.

In praise of the senses

What do I know with my eyes? I am a child today, lost in fog. Mist spatters my car windows; it's difficult to breathe. Chimes in wind. Musical bracelets. Perfumed hands more chemical than flower. In the mirror, my eyes are innocent. Marbled and grave. On the anniversary of really looking. I never heard buzzing till the lights were dimmed. My mouth tastes dull and old, the gray of tepid water. Air hisses through swollen cavities. Pen presses its indentation into my middle finger, a palpable effort of words. I wear this mark. I hold so hard. Try as it might, sun can't push through. Not this day. I see what I see. The rest sloughs off. I teeter on the border of the tangible.

In praise of borders

Some days, it is impossible to trespass boundaries of skin, ineluctable schism between container and what's uncontainable. Some days, this brain is on its knees in gratitude for lines of demarcation. Clean distinctions: beginnings / ends. Other days I kick up dust, scuff my soles, obliterate all ruled measures. Question is always: on which side are you going to live? I pledge allegiance to the amorphous, to amorous morphing of adherence to principle. I declare my residence on ever-shifting margins of society, out beyond all limits of propriety. Forgive my leaping molecules, landing this way and that, water on a hot griddle. This dance of illegal ingress / egress. Who is me now and is that your hand?

In praise of hands

Your hands are not the symphony I fall asleep to in pre-dawn hours. Dawn is not a shiver traveling my spine. Spine is not a ladder on which monkeys climb to heaven. A ladder is no teacup on a winter afternoon. Winter is not the crack through which the world opens. Lines in your palms are not rivers of the Underworld. Door to the Underworld does not open just because I knock there. A symphony is not a dictionary of lost memory. Lost memory of touch does not flower in my garden. Flowers are not the provender of monkeys. Your splayed fingers are not keepers of secrets. Cupped palms not dispensers of favor. Every hour is not divided into blunt heartbeats. Sleep is neither refuge nor root. Heaven is not a shattered teacup in your hands.

In praise of heaven

It's the last place you should look for me. Cotillion on the head of a pin. More likely you'll find me in the circle of the irreducible. It's eternal rest I pine for but my nerves can't tolerate. "You can rest when you're dead" — what if that's false advertising? Stuck at the tollbooth of the afterlife. "Exact change only." Can't remember exactly where I took that wrong turn, too stubborn to ask directions. *Do you know the way to San Jose?* There's a tune I keep humming, can't remember where I heard it. Maybe it's a dream that broke open when the alarm foreclosed night. I keep looking east for the morning star, but sky's gone crazy purple. Hoofbeats in my veins; horsemen leave me in a cloud of dust on the day after. Then everybody's gone, and I'm alone, at last, wandering this forgotten planet, this burned up star in resurrection's wake.

In praise of resurrection

Receive me now from the place where for so long I've sojourned. Everyone deserves a second chance. Sew me new skin for the long journey. Underneath, I'll wear the bruises I was born with. Rescue past from its ignominious tomb, unmarked sepulcher of the unknown and undercounted. Release prisoners from their hand-forged cells. Exchange guilty for innocent. Charge the devout with oblivion. Triumphant, we re-enter the vanquished citadel. Instead of a parade, we come upon the end of the world. Only cripples and lepers stand at roadside, toothless jaws gaping, to watch our return from the precipice on which they tremble. No one remembers how or why; no one remembers nothing.

In praise of nothing

It is harder to hold breath out than to hold it in, harder to sustain that emptiness, be full of nothing. It's fear of death, the Master instructs. But death is *something*, isn't it? Zero is to have never been. No story. No hero. No matter what you add to aught, it comes up *nada*. Void leers. Billboard declares, "You'll rest when you're dead." I know it's talking to me. Mantra wakes me at 4 a.m. I have to remind myself to breathe. White noise of my mind is a busy freeway. It's always rush hour. Everyone breaks speed limit, changes lanes, breaks sound barrier. Helicopters overhead travel at speed of light. Why fight? My bookshelves are overrun, files teem. Credit maxed out. Bathroom cabinet chockablock with lipsticks. We're wired for excess, not dearth. But "not enough" is not nothing. Nothing has its own mathematics. Hole in the world through which I never stop falling, nothing to read the whole way down.

In praise of reading

Words spill into my eyes like rain. A book is a doorway to another world. Another and another. Always I am slipping through, escaping my disappearing landscape. Layers of omniscience obscuring my own blank view. Accreting instead of shedding skin. Callus or scar tissue. I construct myself from shards of paragraphs. I am a fiction. Books are the poor person's world tour; luggage is light. Vistas I've seen from the prow of a book—they've entered my dreams, re-patterned my breath, made me forget my native tongue. Fingertips dry as paper. Paper the lover to whom I am betrothed. Signature bound. Library our chapel, temple to whatever the human hand could record. Monument to words' broken and clumsy attempt to erect meaning. We worship even when we cannot understand. Lie down on the altar, then. Take up the scripture. Let text flood iris like a summer storm.

In praise of storm

All night, restless fingertips on roof. I can't stop shaking. Or is it the sky? I awaken to the world streaming. Is it my eyes? Barometer plummets. Wind chimes frantic on the front porch. Landscape disappeared. Headlights at noon. Umbrellas gutted, skinny ribs exposed. With each squall, I grow nostalgic for the storms of memory. Before the climate changed. With each tempest, I grow more twitchy, hydroplaning on the submerged pavement of my life. Even the least reverent among us bows to weather. We want to imagine it familiar, someone to be reckoned with—the celestial bowler scoring nothing but strikes, the muscled hurler of zigzag thunderbolts. How else can we keep the roof on, maintain the illusion things are under our control?

Terry Wolverton

In praise of control

I want to own the way you understand me. Blind moments when you find me. Choreograph the map of sunlight's slant, placement and intensity of shadow. I want to tunnel through your dark canal, wallow in chambered crenellations, wet words. Let birds break into your brain, rearrange its crumbling monuments, render penitent the listless id. Mad to insist on broken wristed hand signals, wan trickle of losses passes from yesterday to tomorrow. No sorrow's dam can hold back the flood. Blood red tarot devil weeps, survival seeps his prediction into my shaken predilection. Dust. How must I train you to translate me, bear me to heaven in a woven bowl, tongue the rain sieve of my wayward soul?

In praise of soul

Is it in the bass or the rhythm section, distinction between Motown and Philadelphia soul? Does it smolder in hips or pout on thin lips of white girls grown envious of subjugation? Who perm their silky hair. Who scan their features for a map of Africa. They too want to don hot pants of righteousness, uncover an ancientness suburbs scrub clean. I remember soul train. Shadow angels on station platform waving us off in whistle and steam. Night gleam past windows, worlds abandoned to blur. Way my thoughts obscure when my hips wail. Grip dark with long, lacquered fingernails. Bury my bones in psychedelic shack. Jump back. Try to boogaloo, white girl, sad like a bad driver.

The galaxy in praise of bad drivers

Stars swoop from my spiraling arms as I swirl through space. Am I place or container, swollen with gasses and mystery, elemental rock and flame, and no small number of bad drivers? Those whose unintended turn signals blink indecipherable messages to my nether regions. Ones whose constant depression of brake seems destined to disprove inertia. Those whose junkers become a shuddering wall of bass. Speed junkies, hell bent to get there first. Ones who defy law that proclaims, "Two bodies cannot occupy the same space at the same time." Trancemobiles on autopilot, who demonstrate the fallibility of physics. Who believe, touchingly, they are alone in freeway's universe, cheerfully oblivious to their place in the constellation.

In praise of constellations

I praise things that don't exist. Or only in the mind's imagination. Bear. Archer. Dipper. Virgin. Eyes' sleight-of-hand, assembling coins of cosmic dust into recognizable shape. Pre-frontal cortex a magician of light. Presto—mystery becomes mundane, vastness morphed into the familiar. Once form is named, not-form disappears; thus we invent our way to grasp. Brain cannot perceive what it can't classify. What else might we have missed? Meanwhile, we cling to comfort of known tropes. Look at your own life: On what green wheel of illusion do you spin?

In praise of green

Opposite of kiss is green, and it burns in the meadow of the dead. Green hops a train into the heart of night, until it comes to doze by a fire, its plate of cake untouched. At five, my birthday cake was frosted with nothing but time, airless hours that rested heavy as a kiss in my slumbering heart. No fence to shield me, skin pregnable as cloud. In dead meadow, time is a cloud on fire. That train hurtles through airless hours. Green the lost language of slumbering flowers in the heart of night. My untouched skin, straw flowers for the dead, heavy as day-old cake.

In praise of flowers

Flowers wilt while I wait. My smile is plaster. I wear a lonely dress. White ladies croon to lost continents, promises someone must have meant, didn't they? My rings are Saturn. When will it be Tuesday? I keep waiting for stars to erupt. Rain petals. No surprises in the grape jelly of our days. Flowers beg for an opening. When the animals come for us, I will dress in gray rags, walk in the devastated garden through caverns of longing. I can't admit the moment has ended. No scent lingers in the crook of her neck. We stop the fire. Scatter seeds in the ash. Tomorrow I won't remember the map of my continent, smart waste of this transitory star.

In praise of waste

I seldom rise to greet the men who hoist my refuse into maws of bright green trucks. Yet their engine's music summons me from dreams, terrible whine of gears, then resonance of metal digesting. It is night when I prepare my gift for them, intricately sort plastic bottles, aluminum foil, forest of junk mail from bones and rinds and seeds. So tenderly I wrap twist ties, offer my prayer they'll be secure, withstand the scrutiny of the street. That flimsy, barely opaque skin contains evidence I want no one to see—what's used up, cast off, disclaimed by me. History sheathed in polyethylene. It seems so vulnerable, slumped at the curb. My pale doppelganger.

In praise of my doppelganger

Without warning, she forgets her place, occupies my skin, stretches it like a cheap sweater. It's her voice I hear past midnight as I sit before my cathode ray tube and knit my skein of worry. She's an empty pocket, whole allowance blown on tawdry souvenirs—their tinsel flakes into my fingerprints. She enters the conversation like a ghost word, worms through crust of meaning, turns tongue to cotton. She borrows my dreams, returns them smudged, broken. She wears me like a shield. Still, it is her arms into which I roll each night, her pulse that ticks through darkness until morning. She who is the gateway to my dreams. If only she'd stop farting in bed or learn a few new jokes.

Terry Wolverton

In praise of jokes

Two musicians are driving when they notice the Grim Reaper in the back seat. Why do bald people put holes in their pockets? The CIA had an opening for an assassin. Why don't cannibals eat clowns? A guy comes walking into a bar with a turtle on his head. A man has a dog that snores in his sleep. A farmer has 200 hens and no rooster. A frog telephones the Psychic Hotline. How do you make a blonde laugh on Saturday? Descartes is sitting in a bar, having a drink. Adam was walking around the garden of Eden, moping. A boy prayed for two weeks for $100 but nothing happened. What does an atheist say when she's having an orgasm? A woman is learning to golf. A petty thief, a teacher, and lawyer die and go to heaven. A distraught man goes to see a psychologist. Adolf Hitler went to see a fortune-teller. How many surrealists does it take to change a light bulb? Doctor, doctor, I have 59 seconds to live.

In praise of living

Man in white tutu over his jeans dances in downpour on Sunset Boulevard. Legs whirl, face stretched to sky. L.A. on storm watch. Rain today falls green. Any moment can yield the absurd. Something to be said for the adventure of it. Brave because tragic. Tragic because we fall for our illusions. Though I confess, the alternative appeals: exhale, energy released to ether, exploded star. Bags packed; *I'm ready to go anytime.* But I stick around for the punch line. The miracle. Woman chattering to herself in musical French in crowded aisles of Nature Mart like a bird before light. Buying yams, lima beans. Buoyed by sparks, the pulse persists persists persists. Its rhythm steady in the rain.

In praise of rhythm

Close my eyes, words disappear. Reveal breath's incessant prayer. Expose the heartbeat's disrepair. Heal the pulsing hemisphere. Music of the inner ear. *Before meaning comes the sound. Before meaning comes the sound. Torn keening of the drowned. Born dreaming underground.* Eat beat. Complete beat. Secrete beat. Bittersweet beat. Overheat beat. Words splinter into syllables. Plosives, liquids, aspirates. Blurred cinders in a caves of skulls. Birds jitter into still repose. Words rendered, left to decompose. Steal one as a souvenir. Preening in the aural mirror. Close my eyes.

In praise of mirrors

Everything mirrored is reversed; how can I trust what I see? Child dances before her reflection, sings of angels. One silvered surface shows me bloated, sensuous; another reveals a lazy rectitude. In the glass of redemption: only a wisp of smoke. Shadow is one kind of mirror. X-ray, another. Each a facet of truth, but not truth. Anything can be a mirror: clear lake reverberating sky, pure black dinner plate, splayed palm of my hand, graffiti'd cinderblock wall, the newspaper. Woman in mirror looks like me, but older. Each of us a copy of the other—which is original? Angel tangos before her reflection, sings of lost dolls. See what I can trust? Verse and reverse: mirrored everything.

In praise of everything

Plastic trolls with lime green hair. Chia Pets and ThighMasters. Fruitcake and acrylic nails. Televangelists. Push-up bras, thong panties. Men who ask, "Who's your Daddy?" Shock jocks. Christmas Muzak. HoHos and DingDongs. Bikini wax. Ads for antidepressants. Las Vegas. Stuffed crust pizza and a Diet Coke. Grand Theft Auto. SUVs. Botox and liposuction. Nuclear proliferation. Creationism. Chemical peels. Crystal meth. School prayer. Superstores. Cell phone in a crowded theater. People who say, "Not in my backyard." Pierced nipples. Penis enlargement. Soccer moms and deadbeat dads. Dog sweaters and Baby Gap. In vitro fertilization. Gangsta' rap. *Mantra wakes me at 4 a.m. I have to remind myself to breathe*. Traffic on the 405.

In praise of traffic on the 405

Wheels tell wind who gone. It's always rush hour on the 405. One hour seeps into next, steady exodus from north to south and back again. We yearn to go, but freeway holds us earthbound, suspended. Rush hour is not happy hour. Ten wide lanes of momentum thwarted, unasked for stay. Deprived of destination. Captive witness to vistas beyond the glass: hoods of broken-downs gaping like beaks of giant metal birds, brutal ballets of collision, fire scorching up the stretch of hillside, woman in the front seat screaming. But it's not rush hour that makes us scream. Traffic lubricates, allows this sound to erupt from the dark prison where we keep it locked, buoys it past the iron gate of our lips. Without this unscheduled pause for screaming, we would implode. Roll down your window and sing.

In praise of singing

How many times must I try to explain that song is necessary to the soul, even tuneless melodies where one's voice warbles and wavers like a tightrope walker on the verge of misstep. No one says, "That bird is off-key and I must shoot it to shut it up." Each bird has its own song, and we understand none of them. A whole sky borne universe eludes our ill-tuned ears. What if God speaks in the language of birdsong? What instructions have we missed? Wind sweeps through the larynx of the world; all is vibrating, even if we can't feel it. It resounds in the cathedral of my skull, painful imitations of more perfect notes that exist in pure theory. Still, my flawed throat opens; prayer erupts.

In praise of prayer

Pray for a parking space. Pray that she'll call. Pray the publisher says yes. That the test results are negative. That tonight he won't come home smashed. Pray you won't run out of gas. Pray for the hostages. To sleep through the night. His death will be painless. That someday, they'll understand. Listen. Right now, someone, somewhere, is praying for you. Knees pressed to dirt or carpet. Concrete or rock. Eyes closed or open. Hands at heart or forehead to floor. Whether or not you know his name. Whether or not you want her to. Someone is writing you a new future. Can you feel the balm of intention enter your atmosphere like a fragrant breeze? Or hot breath on the back of your neck? Or is it a hum, like power lines, that alters your magnetic frequency? Someone erases your past, renders you unborn. Your nerves crackle all day.

In praise of the unborn

Outside my window, the unborn leer at me. Clutching their tiny picket signs scrawled with obscenities. Lost notes of music from other times. I can't think where I put my eyeballs. All blurred children ask questions in song. Tell lies in pictures scratched in chalk on garage doors that face the treacherous alley. They scatter at sound of creaking hinge. Sewn from patterned cloth at birth, stitched too tight or scarcely basted, we keep shitting ourselves but no one comes to change us. What is the music of latency? We read with eyes we don't know we possess. Finger the Braille of future. Count unsprouted seed. Coyote bones told me a story I didn't want to hear. Are we unborn until we're born again? Insert the eyeballs backward so I might see inside. I've fallen so much it feels like flying now.

In praise of flying

I feel at home in airports, wistful monuments to the forgotten 20th century. Nostalgia of glass and metal, of progress, momentum. I thrill to embarkation: Sliding doors part. Curb's chaos abandoned for aesthetics of beige and steel. Inside, it is always fluorescent daytime; weather always air-conditioned. I observe the pre-flight rituals: Place phone call from a bank of payphones, tell someone goodbye. Buy a newspaper from someplace else, hope news is better there. Browse gift shop for unexpected treasure. Make an offering to the nun collecting for orphans; this ensures safe travel. Sit on leatherette in blue lit bar, watch planes tilt toward horizon. I wrap myself in anonymity like a cashmere shawl, prepare to journey. My passport photo does not match my face. Upon arrival, I might be anyone.

In praise of anyone

When the trains leave, they don't come back. Gypsy train, take me someplace I've never been, someplace unmapped. I have a fondness for finger cymbals and dollar bills. Always I am kneading time, watch it rise, pummel it down again. I have a fistful of coins but no salvation awaits. My mother hops a train to the night carnival. It is her last moment to herself, dark vein pulsing under her left eye; she looks pale, as Midwesterners do in winter. On holidays, I walk alone through empty city, heels mark time against pavement; ghost waiter serves me dinner in a quiet restaurant. I walk home to find a tsunami in the living room, tomorrow breaking heave and swell over my life. Expectations carried out to sea. I will not be an eggshell. This, my undiscovered gift.

In praise of eggshells

All night I am tap tap tapping on walls that encompass me, knuckles searching for a spot to break through. Some flaw in this perfect design. Yet I cling to my smooth cave, its porous walls, essence of chalk and limestone, coral and pearls. Cherish the cool white façade I present to passersby. Few even hear the heartbeat inside. Here I can hide, unopened. Latent and unexamined. A mystery. Still, my shape contorts in ovoid boundaries. each day a little more cramped. Some part of me has not forgotten I can be free; this prison designed to be self-shattering, intended to facilitate escape. But the other part refuses to quit this brittle preservation, croons in the gelid womb, sucks its thumb. Waits. Knows this house will rupture on its own someday, despite its shuttered windows, despite its curtains of denial.

About the Author

Terry Wolverton is the author of five books: *Embers*, a novel in poems; *Insurgent Muse: life and art at the Woman's Building*, a memoir; *Bailey's Beads*, a novel; and two collections of poetry: *Black Slip* and *Mystery Bruise*. A new novel, *The Labrys Reunion*, is forthcoming from Haworth Press. She has also edited thirteen literary anthologies, including  *Mischief, Caprice, and Other Poetic Strategies*. She is the founder of Writers At Work, a creative writing center in Los Angeles, where she teaches fiction and poetry.